P9-EDR-616

THE Improbable Swervings of Atoms

PITT POETRY SERIES

Ed Ochester, Editor

Christopher Bursk

THE
Improbable
swervings
of
A toms

UNIVERSITY OF PITTSBURGH PRESS

The publication of this book is supported by a grant
from the Pennsylvania Council on the Arts

PENNSYLVANIA
COUNCIL
ON THE
ARTS

Published by the University of Pittsburgh Press, Pittsburgh, PA 15260

This book is the winner of the 2004 Donald Hall Prize in Poetry, awarded
by the Association of Writers and Writing Programs. AWP, a national
organization serving over three hundred colleges and universities, has its
headquarters at George Mason University, Mail Stop 1E3, Fairfax, VA 22030.

This book is dedicated to Jake, Zack, Josie, Tyler,
and Maggie Ann, those irresistible swervings of atoms

and in memory of Ray Reilly, Peg Stevens, Richard Sivel,
and Amanda Sancataldo

I'd like to remind you again how porous
Things are—as I made clear in my first book.

Lucretius, De Rerum Natura, Book Six

Another fact I wish you to know:
When the atoms are carried straight down through the void
By their own weight, at an utterly random time
And a random point in space they swerve a little,
Only enough to call it a tilt in motion
For if atoms did not tend to lean, they would
Plummet like raindrops through the depths of space,
No first collisions born, no blows created,
So Nature never could have made a thing.

Lucretius, De Rerum Natura, Book Two

Contents

1

Well, if to have a living, sensing creature
We have to grant the atoms all its sense,
What of the atoms that make people grow?
They'd be struck by something funny, I guess,
     and they'd shake
With fits of laughter and wet their cheeks with tears;
They'd be so bright they'd discuss the blending of things.
No, more, they'd delve into their own beginnings . . .

De Rerum Natura, Book Two

Freedom Train

Because my mother, in her nightgown,
started wandering into neighbors' houses and explaining
how easy it'd be to drown a child,
and because my father loved diesel engines,
he thought a train trip might be good for us all.
That year, the Bill of Rights and Mayflower Compact
were riding in glass cabinets

from city to city. We caught up with the Constitution
in Wilmington, Delaware. My father had timed it
exactly so we'd step off the midnight special
and onto the Freedom Train
the morning before it pulled out and headed for its next
stop. There'd been a war and now
there wasn't a war, and the original manuscript
of Monroe's Manifest Destiny
was right in front of me and people were pressing
against me, and my father was saying, *Look! Look!*

and I knew that in the cramped, hot air inside the Pullman car
he expected me to explode
into so many syllables of delight
they'd make the whole trip worthwhile,
but I couldn't do anything but stare.
It was what I'd learned to do

while my mother, weeping, rubbed salve
into the scratches she'd made on my cheek and my arm:
I paid attention to dust on a sill,
the frayed ends of rope,
a raindrop not quite ready to commit itself
to plunging down a window.

Here was Jefferson's draft of the Declaration of Independence
and the Treaty of Paris
and the Emancipation Proclamation
and the best I could do
was to tighten and open my fists inside my pockets.
What was my father to do with a boy like me?

Army Hearings

One day my father brought home a large box of polished wood
with glass in front and rooms inside
that had sea serpents, witches, and cowboys
and a man who played the ukulele
and women who cried when crowns were laid on their teased hair,
and to go into each room you didn't open a door
but turned a knob. Each day after school
Beany and Cecil and Kukla, Fran, and Ollie and Buffalo Bob
would talk to my brothers and me.
Then one afternoon there was only a head
so large I grew afraid
that it would burst the sides of the television.
It talked the way I imagined a rock would
if it dressed up in blue serge and sat
in front of a microphone and pointed its finger
at professors and lawyers and generals
till they shrank
inside their shirts. How did they get so small
and the man so big? I'd come home
from school and adjust the rabbit ears
and think, okay, he's got to be gone by now,
but on every channel he'd bellow
the way I thought only fathers did
when they got too tired
to love you anymore, or teachers
when they tried to make you ashamed for not knowing
as much as they did. So this is what words could do:
get people to squirm, sweat, loosen their ties, look down
at their hands. So this is what happened
when you got older. I watched
the way you might a snake about to strike.
What was the point of moving?
It would be like shutting the closet door and hoping to
hide in a house full of flames.
Eventually the fire would get around to me.

One More Victory for the Children of Light,
One More Defeat for the Children of Darkness

A dozen Arabs cost $3.95 a box
so I had to slaughter the same men
over and over. Day after day
they disregarded common sense and charged the line of fire,
pure zeal once more trying to
overcome howitzers and turn away bullets aimed
for their hearts. Their flowing capes
gave their horses wings
and the horses' manes gave the riders the courage
to fly over any rampart. They rose
with the muscular assurance of birds of prey
and headed straight for the same weak spot
in Her Majesty's Royal Soldiers, a kid
so slender he could be mistaken for a girl,
his hands soldered to his drum
so he had to keep up the call to arms
even after spears were driven
into him, steel plunged again
and again into the hole I'd made in his chest
with my father's screwdriver. If it took ten minutes
to kill him, it took much longer
to mourn him, a pink-cheeked lad
so beloved by every man in his regiment, so martyred
there could be no hope
for peace now, the whole murderously beautiful Nation of Islam
must pay for the death
of this one boy wrapped in a linen handkerchief
I'd stolen from my mother and offered up
to the earth, a grave so deep
I wasn't sure I could find him
the next day. I had no idea what was going on
in Egypt or the Sudan or Palestine,
but in my playroom's shadows good never triumphed
without cost.

Dr. Livingstone, I Presume

It may have been 1951 in every home in America
but in ours it was 1865 and my brother and I were going to do
what no human had
yet dared: on the backs of elephants carry Christ
into the jungle and diamonds out.
All we needed were machetes, some quinine, and an excuse
and we'd conquer the Congo.
Who better understood mosquitoes than us?
It didn't daunt my brother
that we'd never bicycled past the town limits.
What was fording a few rapids
compared to battling space aliens for the right
to stake a flag into the red dust of the next-door planet?
This time we'd have gravity
on our side. Nothing's easier
than murdering a whole tribe if you've got guns
that don't have to be reloaded
right away and also a proclamation from the president
and pamphlets from the Aborigines Relief Society
and an open market for all the ivory you can hack
off the corpses of creatures who'd evolved
so children in Schenectady could play a little Brahms
and London barristers might chew meat again,
all because of my brother and me
and a few thousand natives born in the wasteful squalor
of the jungle. How could we not punish the heathens
for dropping things along the trail and dying
at the very moment Western civilization most needed them
to bear the burdens with which they'd been entrusted?
At least we weren't Arabs or Catholics or Huns.
For our gardens we'd not make a border
of the natives' severed heads,
nor cut off their sons' hands. We'd not even whip our slaves
unless we had to. We were Americans.

We wouldn't kill anyone
unless they asked for it,
and it grieved us when they did
again and again.

My Brother and I Drop the Bomb on Hiroshima

How else do you teach morality to aphids?
Of course, it wasn't beetles we were spraying,
but the principle's the same. And we were principled,
my brother and I. Every afternoon
we shot down kamikaze pilots.
It was like trying to swat wasps in the air.
Finally you have no recourse but to attack the hive;
show other wasps what their fate would be.
If you keep getting stung, you go to the source.
You can't be subtle with bugs.
So we blew up not just one city but two.
We didn't bomb the children
merely because we wanted to observe the skin peel
off their faces, their hair
come out in their hands. But their fathers and sons
had refused to die. So it was up to us
to rescue the world even if a little girl had to
watch her grandfather's eyeballs dissolve.
That was his own fault for being born
ignorant enough to look up
into the sky at the very moment our bomb chose
to reveal itself in all its glory,
the rivers swarming with people
in what proved to be nothing less than a mass baptism,
the streets lush with blossoms opening
as if the bombs had triggered in the flowers
a recognition of kindred beauty. It's always glorious
when something you've planted
takes seed and blossoms.

Nothing More Dangerous than Boredom

1

There's only so much you can do
with a chemistry set: magnesium,
nitrogen, phosphorus, iodine. I kept pouring one beaker
into another in the hopes that if I tried this enough times
I'd finally invent something. With a dropper
I squeezed the alphabet
into glass tubes: Fe, Mg, Zn, Ca.
Maybe this was what God did
when he conjured the world: mix
a little sulfur with a little selenium, add a dash
of nickel, a sprinkle of iron —
and presto, majesto! If I couldn't create the earth,
I thought, maybe I'd like to
destroy it. Somebody had to
make it pay for being provisional, makeshift,
doomed. Wouldn't my classmates be surprised
if they knew that I wasn't just running away from them,
I was heading for my laboratory?
I was building a bomb. *Bomb.* The authority
of that word, its alpha and omega.

2

Who'd suspect a boy on a tour of the White House
clutching his winter jacket
and under it more than enough explosives
to blow up not only the Lincoln Bedroom, but the whole West Wing?
I never dreamed of being commander in chief.
Nope, I liked to fantasize
about blowing him up. I didn't hate the president
in particular, but I was tired

of pledging allegiance to anyone who didn't even know
I existed. I'd tried to think like a Boy Scout
but birds and knots weren't interesting enough to fill the hours
between breakfast and dinner.
If I was going to study first aid
I wanted it first hand. I'd read the newspapers
I delivered. Plenty of people had walked into offices and
turned themselves into flames
and legends, bits and pieces
their families wept over. All I needed was the right
blend of chemicals, a triggering
device. Timing, impact, power.
I was eleven. These were always on my mind.

Woodcraft Manual for Boys

The sugar he'd stockpiled before the war
made my grandfather enough fortune to send my father to camp
to learn to undress with other boys, paint
his face, count coups, wager scalps,
make his own bed, and manage
his own finances. Basket-weaving, banking, bartering,
the camp was a model of microeconomics,

boys sent home to their dads bronzed and ready
to balance budgets and subcontract work,
even a kid as skinny as my dad trained to swim
in a lake so cold, he'd brag, years later, refreshing his drink,
that it shriveled the scrotum tight as a golf ball.
Nostalgic for the endless intrigues
of knots, the smell of rope always on the fingers,
fishhooks biting into the soft body of mayfly

after mayfly, my father entreated me
to borrow his *Collected Ernest Thompson Seton* with paw prints
on the covers, the bears apparently having stamped each
volume with their seal of approval,
and though I did love to rub my mother's mascara on me
and wear nothing but my brother's jockstrap
pinned tight and play Indian by myself,

and even though there were no other gifts I knew of
to offer my dad, I still couldn't get interested in books
in which boys managed the unruly workforce
of nature. Nakedness I understood, but not merit badges.
I already suspected that they'd failed my dad.
I remember going to say goodnight to him
and him turning away so I'd get only cheek; tiny, indomitable whiskers,

their fierce determination. It is what I imagined it'd be like
to kiss an Indian warrior: earth
and firewater. I carried to bed the rich malts
of all the scotch my father had drunk that day
so he could sleep that night. I slept
in its pungency, the way another boy, at another time,
might lie down under the heavens
and shut his eyes, knowing that if he opened them
all he'd see would be a darkness someone had loved so much
that he had filled it with stars.

Coffee

Mouths don't empty themselves unless the ear is knowing.

The summer my father and mother broke up
I learned to drink coffee. At first
it was an adventure: to be abandoned
at my great-aunt's house where the only people I met
were servants who drew out their words
till they seemed to be speaking another language
that had no tenses, no worries
about time. That summer I fell in love with Miss Z
whom everyone else feared, the kitchen staff, the gardeners,
even her employer, my great-aunt,
whom she pointedly kept waiting.
Rung for, Miss Z went on sipping her coffee
as if that were her real job: savoring aromas
and telling me stories. *The Turpentine Fields. The Muck.*
The Sugar Cane. Honduras
Where She'd Lain on Her Belly Naked for Two Days
to Become a Witch Doctor.
The Broadway show she'd written, the novel
translated into Dutch and French.
The *Saturday Evening Post* article she unfolded
like a secret document
she'd been hiding just for me, her *little honky*
as she called me, brushing the hair
she insisted I let grow long.
These are my words. All of them.
How could I not believe her
who'd taught me roots: sheepwort, John the Conqueror,
snakevine? She hated every member of the white race
and that summer I hated them too
as I drank my coffee, tasting the extravagance
of that word, its two
double letters. I was thirteen

and allowed to swallow something so dark
and hot it had to be grown-up.
I blew the steam back and forth. It was a spirit
I was training. It would do my bidding.

Fourteen and Under Singles Championship

Hit me. Hit me. I dare you
the ball said as it kept bouncing back up
in Whitey Bremer's face, the way a cartoon duck might
no matter how many times he's shot,
as if the whole point of the hunt is to exasperate
the hunter. While people filled the streets of Damascus
recruited from gyms and wrestling clubs—
the CIA, needing only a few thousand dollars to fund a coup
to depose Musaddiq, and once more
bail out the Shah, Western civilization, and Mobil Oil—
I was overthrowing my own despot, the defending
boys' champion, one year older and almost a foot taller than me.
No matter how often he slugged that little bit of fur
it kept dropping back at his feet.
By the second set he looked about to propel
his whole body across the net. Not just use his racquet
to strike the ball but smash
his fist into my jaw, the way a boxer might
invest all his weight in the next punch, the one that's got to
put an end to the fight. But I refused to be a good sport
and crumble. He'd serve
what should have been ace after ace
and it'd pop back. He'd take my lobs that looked like dirigibles
begging to be shot out of the sky
and hammer them at my groin
only to find them taunting him back on his side of the net.
I was being cruel the only way a skinny kid like me could:
no matter how hard he hit,
I wouldn't beg for mercy, till he was the one
sobbing, flailing, trying to
punish the ball for being made of rubber and bouncing
before him, again and again
as if all his power meant nothing,
all his past victories. It must have been an existential crisis

for the reigning *Fourteen and Under Titlist*
because at last he flung his racquet
to the ground, and in the middle of the thirty-sixth shot
of still another rally, the score tied 12-12,
in front of everyone he'd wanted to be proud of him,
he fled the court, his dad's outstretched arms,
the towel held out by the girl he was sweet on that summer,
the boys he'd bragged to before the match,
and their parents' mumbled condolences,
and I was left standing there
in the summer of the coup of 1953,
on the scarred red clay
looking up at the crowd and realizing
there was no face turned toward me,
no mercy to be had in the world.

Sex Education

My teacher would not let me or anyone in class forget
            that he'd given his right eye in a war
most of us knew little about except
            that some men had ended up brainwashed
and wouldn't come home. I'd seen pictures
            of them in what looked like pajamas
and I'd imagined what it'd be like
            to eat rice all day and hate America,
just as I used to lie in bed and wonder how it'd feel
            to be fondled by strangers
I was always being warned about.
            I'd tried to be the kind of boy
I was supposed to be—*upstanding, loyal,*
            trustworthy, reverent, chaste—
but just before sleep, my hands would go AWOL
            once more, lost in the inscrutable
orient of my groin, its exotic
            spices. I knew that I should turn myself in
to the authorities—though
            ninth-grade Health Studies
didn't seem quite the appropriate place
            to confess, no matter how often
the teacher invited questions. My wandering mind
            or my wandering fingers?
Which was the worse traitor?
            All through class I drew pictures
of bamboo cages where the prisoners were American
            and couldn't help liking
the way they felt their bodies moving
            inside their loose prison jammies,
the way light fell on this other side
            of the world, the lure

of another language; its nouns' and verbs'
       foreign customs, the sudden
compulsion to beg forgiveness for all
       the sins of their country.

The Barbarians

> We face a hostile ideology, global in scope, atheistic in charac-
> ter, ruthless in purpose, and insidious in method.
>
> Dwight David Eisenhower, January 17, 1961

My body was already being invaded by an army
I could no more stop than the Romans could
the Visigoths. Stamp out a few
and more popped up. And Eisenhower was worried
about the Communists? I was at the mercy
of vandals, thousands upon thousands
of pillagers with no history
and, therefore, no scruples, even the most private parts of me
under siege, no matter how vigilant I was
patrolling borders. If I looked away for just a moment
I found myself being plundered
anew, the horde back, preoccupied
with doing what a horde is good at.
Whole tribes set up camp in my armpits,
in my groin, digging in roots so deep
it would have been suicide to try
to eradicate them, my body not mine anymore
to do with as I wished.
I ought to have been a good Roman,
imperturbable in the midst of the squalor,
yet here I was:
picking at, scrubbing, swabbing, swathing, trying to
pluck each rebellious hair. No part of me
off-limits: chest, belly, scrotal sac.
*What's wrong with me? What's wrong
with me?* Even that stalwart defender
of the faith, my penis, had turned
native, traitor, aboriginal
and mutinous. Would nothing ever be safe
from the barbarians?

DE RERUM NATURA, Book Five

> Harsh Discord thus makes one thing out of another,
> Horrible weapons . . . increasing day by day the terror of war.
> They even tested bulls in the thick of battle
> And drove wild boars against the enemy.

The wild boars may not have known their Latin
but they had other talents. They didn't care what flag
they followed, they gored
equally their masters' foes and their masters
who had presumed to think
that the guided missiles they'd launched, this latest leap
forward in military science, harnessed
hogs, wouldn't dream
of veering off course and heading straight back
for the very masterminds who'd unleashed them,
the pigs proving the new technology already
obsolete. No face was left
unmauled, no throat unslashed. It wasn't enough
that the men died; they had to be punished
further, breasts ripped open, testicles
devoured. Lucretius spares no
details; he takes his time just as the lion did
drinking from the opened chest of the lion tamer,
one more case of the experiment
getting revenge on the experimenter.
Had some general thought to tame nature so utterly
that he could persuade leopards into choosing sides, throw reins
over ocelots, talk lynxes into enlisting?
They might have made it out of boot camp,
but in the battlefield, blood
was blood, and so they did their own recruiting.
If the light artillery backfired,
so did the heavy: elephants, walking nuclear bombs,
moving forts, grew weary
of being nothing but huge
moments in history, and wandered off, dragging

bodies behind them like footnotes.
The bulls got it into their thick heads that they deserved better
than being weapons, and, whipped into battle,
threw off their riders, trampled them so thoroughly
men turned into slurry under the beasts' hooves.
One of the bloody scenes that a boy can't help
remembering from Latin IV, that make the long hours
translating a dead language worthwhile.

Irreconcilable Differences

Khrushchev and Eisenhower, that old married couple,
were bickering again, over how often
each could blow up the other,
but I had more pressing matters to deal with:
exactly when and where I'd have a chance to
get Sally Hamilton's blouse unbuttoned.
For weeks I'd been practicing on a bra I'd stolen
from my mother's bureau drawer
and fastened to one dining-room chair
while I sat in another and let the right hand work its way down
to the clasp; it took a while—the thumb standing guard,
the index finger at work, liberating
each hook. Eisenhower and Khrushchev could have learned from me
the virtues of delayed gratification.

If I got an erection just trying it on a dining-room chair,
imagine the ecstasy of doing it
with a real girl, stroking an actual nipple.
Should I devote my attention to both breasts? Or
lavish my affections on one
at a time? Unlike the president I didn't have a cabinet of advisors.
When the U-2 went down,
and the Soviet premier carried on like an aggrieved wife,
Eisenhower fidgeted like one more henpecked husband
caught cheating but doing his best
to make it seem as if it weren't the end of the world.

I had even more complicated negotiations
to see to: how to place one important part
of my body into an equally important part
of a girl's body. Talk about the need for diplomacy!
I had my hands full. What did my penis know
of tact, my greedy upstart, ugly American
determined once again to meddle

in someone else's internal affairs? I had a weapon
I needed to test, bombs I was tired
of stockpiling, and I intended to drop one wherever
and whenever I could—just to see how much
of an explosion it would make
and if I could survive the blast.

One Nation, Indivisible, Under God

On the day that the St. Lawrence Seaway opened
for saltwater ships to sail deep into the heart of America,
I was being launched into water too,
my head stuck in the toilet
thanks to the good offices of the student council
vice president, the class treasurer, and the captain
of the volleyball team, all of whom decided
that if I wasn't a faggot, I ought to be. Last week
it'd been my best friend's turn, but luckily today
they'd been kind enough not to
piss in the toilet beforehand. They were doing me a favor,
one boy told me, as another
laid his hands on my head, the way a pastor might
press down a reluctant parishioner
into the baptismal font again
and again, as if once wasn't enough
to cleanse a soul. Each time my face hit the water
it seemed to mock me. Each time
my head was yanked up,
my mouth tried to swallow
enough air for when I'd be pushed down
again. I was already worrying
about how I'd explain to my dad why I'd come home
reeking of disinfectant. What I remember most
are the arms of the eleventh-grade
treasurer, holding me from behind so tightly
he could have been hugging me,
the minty breath of the volleyball captain
as he pressed my head into the toilet,
the hands of the just-elected vice president
on the back of my neck
as if he were trying to teach me to swim
the only way he knew how.

E Pluribus Unum

Just what's going on in that thick skull
of yours? asks the teacher and it takes you a while to figure out
that he's talking to you, and though you're tempted
to tell him that you are, in fact, contemplating
United States history, you don't
because football practice is next
and what is going through your head
is a locker room full of naked presidents,
all the Jameses and Johns showering together.
When you got on the school bus this morning
you didn't plan to think about Grover Cleveland
scrubbing Chester Arthur's back,
or Millard Fillmore letting his towel fall away
so there's no mistaking his most democratic part,
or Monroe scratching his balls
as if that were his manifest destiny. How is a boy to explain
that he's got John Quincy Adams's testicles
on his mind and Warren Harding's buttocks?
When Thomas Jefferson bends over
you can almost see into the darkness
that fills the third president of the United States.
What did you expect? That George Washington
would be all padding like your grandmother?
Did you doubt that a man in a wig
would have the same parts as you, more
or less? Poor penis,
who wouldn't wish to comfort such a wobbly thing
no matter what wars it waged, whom it managed
to exterminate? Teddy Roosevelt's can't help
saluting to the Republic. Eisenhower's just lolls there
as if it's earned the right to do nothing
presidential for a while. What hope is there for you
if this is the kind of thing you're going to imagine:
Rutherford B. Hayes letting the water

have its way with him,
Woodrow Wilson drawing faces in the steam on the mirror
as if even the Leader of the Free World gets tired
of being serious all the time? Today in room 203
all of American history comes down to
a boy thinking things
he shouldn't, and knowing not to say anything, no matter
how hard he's pressed.

You Only Get a Few Chances to Be of Interest to the Gods

When you pulled free from the man's encouraging hands,
when you grabbed for the door,

when you left your coat, sweater, schoolbag in the car's front seat,
when you ran down the street, shirttails flying,

when you crouched in the dark of the first trees you recognized,
when you wiped the spittle from your hands

and began to think of how to explain losing
your algebra book, your pocket atlas, your Latin dictionary,

you knew that you had failed the first real test
of your life. All the man had asked for

was a few moments of undivided attention, kindness
in return for kindness. A kiss.

If a boy is going to be scared of something
that pathetically eager

to please, that naked
and exposed, the penis's trembling

entreaties, how can he expect himself to brave anything
else that the gods might ask of him?

Fortitude. Self-abnegation. Compassion. The valor
of the Latin, the polysyllabics'

magnanimity. You'd been given an opportunity to prove
you too had a large heart

and a deep soul, and you had zipped up your fly
and run for your life.

What Do You Hate about Yourself?

The unmanageable tongue, that slut,
which rubs against anything. With its complete lack
of principles, it insists on making love
to every mucous membrane
it can, worries every cold sore, feasts on any morsel it finds
lodged in the molars, scrap
of beef, dollop of chocolate, the last dark
sweetness of cola. How can a boy explain wanting
to taste everything, even the detergents
of his own body: tears, nose drip, sweat of his armpit, salt
of his wrist, skim milk
of his own semen? No wonder every word's soiled
that comes out of his mouth.
Walking home from football practice or his job at the dairy
he may try to disguise his voice, pick a fight
with the dark, talk
as he imagines the trees might, speak only
in their deep voices. But it's no good,
soon he will be back to his old habits:
serenading a cat on a stone wall,
singing opera to the clouds, falsetto,
then bass, then falsetto again, then bass.
Lothario and jilted lover,
one minute heartless, the next minute heartbroken,
now deceiver, now brutally deceived.
O throat, you have betrayed me again.
O mouth, can you never be trusted?

2

Now you see all this discord in the bronze
Is caused when a first wave of the bronze-atoms
Seizes and occupies the open highways
In the iron, but then a troop comes from the magnet,
Finds all the ways full, finds nowhere to wade, as before.
Then it's forced to give that iron mesh a knocking
And pound it away with its tides. So, through the bronze,
It spits back what it would suck in without it.

De Rerum Natura, Book Six

That'll Be the Day

Before my father brought home the future
governor of Massachusetts
my brothers and I were coached on how to shake hands
with a grip firm enough
to impress Churchill. It'd be like sitting down to dinner
with History, my father said.
Luckily, History was too well-bred
to remark on my bad manners.
Sixteen and fed up with diplomacy, I fled, eager
to get back to what mattered:
Fats Domino, Chuck Berry, Little Anthony and the Imperials.
While my progenitor and the soon-to-be
candidate for vice president
talked corporate incentives and tax breaks
I turned up my radio
and kept *I found my thrill on Blueberry Hill*
blaring, even after
being asked politely to turn it down.
My father took pains not to lift his voice
in front of guests,
but I sang at the top of mine.
I had my old man just where I wanted him:
Walking the Dog.
Chains of Love.
Maybe I'd drive History crazy also.
Maybe it'd grow sick of hearing the same words
over and over. Maybe
I'd get a rise out of it too:
Wake up, little Susie! Wake up!
Everyone had a breaking point,
and I was going to see what History's was.

Mutually Assured Destruction

Go into the locker room at halftime in almost any high school
in this nation and there's so much paranoia
it'd make the CIA proud. Harvard-trained agents
might be working out the details of how to lace Castro's coffee
with cyanide or rig an exotic conch shell
with enough explosives to blow up the skin-diving dictator,

but *our* coach was plotting just as furiously—
flank attacks, forays, ambushes, incursions,
the point of the game not to beat a team
but demolish it, drive your helmet hard
into throat or thigh, punish a kid for having a belly
or groin, for being soft
anywhere. Faced with an infestation,

you don't think twice about the morality of getting rid of bugs,
you squash them by any means necessary.
Not even the mouth was safe.
It had to have rubber stuck between the teeth.
It was the practice before the game on which
our whole season and, we were led to believe, our lives
depended. So why was I unstrapping my helmet and laying it down
the way one might a baby on a doorstep

though even that didn't seem enough? So I took off my jersey,
my shoulder-pads, my tee-shirt, all that foam and plastic
needed to hit someone
with the blessing of principal, school, the entire town.
I lifted off my back every blocked punt, fumble recovery
every tackle I'd ever made, four years
of scrimmages. At the fifty-yard line I knelt,
untied my shoes, peeled off my two pairs of socks.

No one moved, coaches, teammates. I knew no one in the world
who'd approve of what I was doing.
And yet still I unlaced my pants
and stepped out of them, folded them carefully
—I owed my uniform that much—
let my hip-pads drop to the ground, right beside the goalposts.

Then, as if not till utterly naked would I know what to do next,
I tugged off my jockstrap, crazy
slingshot, invention so odd it was worthy of the CIA,
and in front of everyone I let the air touch me
anywhere it wished. Now I belonged to no one
but air and light and time
though my time would hardly be free. I had no idea
what I planned to do with it,
what it planned to do with me.

Why Latin Should Still Be Taught in High School

Because one day I grew so bored
with Lucretius, I fell in love
with the one object that seemed to be stationary,
the sleeping kid two rows up,
the appealing squalor of his drooping socks.
While the author of *De Rerum Natura* was making fun
of those who *fear the steep way and lose the truth*,
I was studying the unruly hairs on Peter Diamond's right leg.
Titus Lucretius Caro labored, dactyl by dactyl,
to convince our Latin IV class of the atomic
composition of smoke and dew,
and I tried to make sense of a boy's ankles,
the calves' intriguing
resiliency, the integrity to the shank,
the solid geometry of my classmate's body.
Light falling through blinds,
a bee flinging itself into a flower,
a seemingly infinite set of texts
to translate and now this particular configuration of atoms
who was given a name at birth,
Peter Diamond, and sat two rows in front of me,
his long arms, his legs that like Lucretius's hexameters
seemed to go on forever, all this hurly-burly
of matter that had the goodness to settle
long enough to make a body
so fascinating it got me
through fifty-five minutes
of the nature of things.

DAS KAPITAL

When my dad extolled the value of money
and got me a job in his friend's factory
so I'd get to experience free enterprise firsthand,

was this what he intended? That I'd grow infatuated
with the face on the twenty-dollar bill, one more
tenderly engraved dead president, his extravagantly

bushy eyebrows, high forehead,
luxurious hair, lock after lock combed like waves
bounding over one another, each

with a score of smaller swirls inside it and each
about to break? Andrew Jackson's eyes never stop
worrying, as if he's just rushed in

from a storm, from staring straight into the wind,
into the face of God,
and the rain has taught him a new kind of grief

for which he'll never find words.
Ah, Karl, ah, Frederick, imagine a country
where thousands and thousands of pictures of this fierce man

circulate, where his inscrutable anguish
can buy a person a steak dinner
or tickets to *South Pacific* or a copy of *Das Kapital*.

Ah, America, where a boy is free to disregard
all of history, the wholesale slaughter
of the Muskogean at Horseshoe Bend, the Negro fort leveled,

and to gaze into the window of a twenty-dollar bill
and find the man of his dreams.

November 29, 1963, LIFE Magazine

A week later, he's still being shot
           in every room of your house.
Even though it takes perhaps a second
           for him to buckle over, the camera
draws out the descent till the distance
           between head and lap
seems as great as that between the window
           a man flings himself out
and the sidewalk he splatters on.
           By the time you're in the bedroom
the president's dead. You've seen people wounded
           in movies, the body doing its best
to accommodate its unexpected
           guest, closing around the bullet
the way members of a family might
           gather around a visitor
to make him feel at home.
           But this is the Leader
of the Free World. Your father
           and mother can't stop
gazing at his corpse. They spread it flat
           on the kitchen table.
They carry it to the bathroom.
           That's the only way they know
to make sense of the death: to
           fill their house with it.
Your sister's face down on her bed,
           nothing left to do
but lie still as one newscaster retraces
           the bullet's path,
another describes the wound. Again
           and again
the body crumples up, grown tired
           of all the work required

just to hold the head in one place.
                    It makes its choice over
and over: collapsing,
                    the only
possibility left it, the only thing
                    it's still free to do.

The Atomic Energy Act of 1962

Things fall apart, that's what the glass said
when I thrust my fist through the window.
That's what the car said
when I drove it into the wall. *Whatever it takes,*
your mother and I are willing to try,
my Dad insisted as he poured another drink.
The scotch rushed into the glass
as if it couldn't bear being cooped up any longer.
It was more than ready
to begin a working relationship with the ice.
If only I had read Lucretius more closely
when I was seventeen, I might have saved my father
thousands of dollars and me
hundreds of hours in therapy. Maybe
instead of *Time* and *Sports Illustrated*
the doctor should have stacked copies of *De Rerum Natura*
in his outer room. Would I have put all that desperate
effort into being seventeen
and normal if I'd thought of myself
merely as atoms
that happened to have a class ranking,
a family history, and a condition listed in the *DSM?*
In the doctor's office the world dissolved
right before my eyes, endless wars
involving millions
of dust motes, their skirmishes in the air,
squadron realignments, broken alliances.

New Year's Resolution

On American Bandstand Jan and Dean are singing *Surf's Up*
and you love the idea of two young men
standing so close you can't tell
whose mouth is making which sound,
and Jan and Dean are both crooning undying love
to the same woman and each is stroking
his hand over the 150 megawatts of electricity
that hang over his crotch. Imagine: beating off
on national television, before scores
of squirming girls and boys. That thought
won't get you a date for the prom. Or early admission
to the college of your choice. Or a starting position
on the baseball team. Or even a pat on the back.
You've got to start concentrating right now
on what you're going to do
for the next forty years of your life instead of going gaga
over a girl two rows up from you in Biology 101
and so gorgeous she puts everything you believe in doubt
because who can major in swooning,
though that's what you do whenever you see certain boys
propel themselves out of their seats and slide down the hall
like battleships being launched
with such fanfare that the water knows to part?
Then you're imagining what it'd be like to bunk
on board one of those ships
named after presidents' wives or movie stars,
though that's probably as close as you will come, you think,
to getting inside a woman. You have no more hopes
of having sexual intercourse with a woman
than you do of getting into Heaven.
Or Harvard. You'd like to
be the jet plane your father launches
into the future, but you can't stop thinking

about the way light falls on the back
of a classmate's neck. You can't even please the doctor
your dad's hired. The doctor wants you to stop worrying
about war in some Southeast Asian country
no one cares about, except the French,
and to start focusing on what really matters.
Okay, you think, now what?

Plymouth Rock

> A proud and very profane young man, one with a lusty, able
> body . . . would always be condemning the poor people in
> their sickness and did not let to tell them that he hoped to
> cast half overboard before they came to their journey's end.
> It was God's providence that he should be the first to die and
> be rolled into the sea—
>
> Book I, Chapter IX, Journal of Gov. Bradford

Concord, Lexington, Salem, Cambridge, Quincy:
I carved *Fuck you* into every tree I could
on the Freedom Trail. I'd been guided through all the circles
of infernal punishment and the worst was Plymouth
Plantation. Since we had the misfortune of living only ten miles
from it, anyone who ever visited my family
got dragged to the famous Rock and there we'd stand,
looking down at it as if it were more
than a large stone with a crack.

What did my mother and father expect?
That the rock would decide to break its silence
and tell all the secrets that it had kept for 310 years?
Maybe that young sailor on the Mayflower, like me, just got fed up
with being on a ship sailing straight into history, its heavy cargo
of saints. Maybe he could see
what kids after him would have to put up with:
Discuss predestination. Define the election of the saints.
Give the key points of the Mayflower Compact.

At four I wet my pants by that rock
and my father got so mad he drove off
without me. At seven, I lost my favorite Flash Gordon key chain
to the tides always cleaning up after the tourists.
At fifteen, I copped my first feel in the mausoleum
built around the very place
the pilgrims first set foot in America. *Grace or Good Works?*

On the road that runs past Plymouth Rock—
with some elderly ladies and a Unitarian minister
and a few other teenagers goofy enough to get up before daybreak—
I held up a sign that read *Honk for Disarmament!*
Stop Nuclear Holocaust! Once a man steered his Buick Cutlass
close enough for his son to lean out
and spit. Then they both roared off, laughing.
Wiping the saliva from my face,
I turned as indignant as any Puritan.
I too wanted that boy to get what was coming to him.
He did. Be assured,
we all do: Jew or Gentile, Conservative
or Orthodox, Loyalist or Patriot, Democrat
or Republican. If history teaches us anything, Pilgrim,
it teaches us that.

Totaled

How could you have been singing one moment
and the next moment have to be helped
to your feet, one cop
on either side of you? You couldn't recall turning
left. You didn't even hear the truck
hit your car till long after it did.
Not till the cops helped you up from the grass and pointed to the car
did you notice your bleeding hands.
You tried to pick up all the pieces
of glass, half of a fender, a door handle, the rearview mirror
Did you think that if you gathered enough parts
you could put the car back together and the last hour
wouldn't have happened? You tore off your shirt
and wrapped it around your friend's wrist.
You got a blanket out of your backseat
for the driver who'd almost killed you
or had you almost killed him? Did you think
that doing everything right
now might make up for all you'd done wrong
just moments ago? You traded insurance cards,
put your signature on the police report
with a flourish the way a leader of a nation might
sign a treaty surrendering lands he'd already lost
in a war. No matter
that you'd remembered to call your grandmother that day,
that you'd lent a friend your calculus notes,
that you'd spent the morning washing dishes at a women's shelter.
No matter how benevolently
the sun had fallen on you just before
you got into the car. Make one blind turn
and you forfeit everything.

Soo-ling

Three months after the president committed troops
to stop Communist encroachment in Southeast Asia
and I lost my virginity and began to suspect
that I might take my place in the world of men
especially as I could drink
my classmates under the table and still get up for my 8 a.m. class,
                                    there I was: president
of the College Literary Society and future Rhodes Scholar
climbing fences, making kissing sounds
as if a cat as thoroughly lost as my mother's
                                    (please note:
my mother's cat, not mine!) would condescend
to be found just because some crazy human was pursing his lips
and making smooching noises
no self-respecting feline or female would ever
acknowledge.
                                    Three weeks before
my father's backyard would fill with businessmen
from South Africa, Indonesia, Turkey,
and I'd shake hands with the Under-Secretary of State,
and show the Attorney General where the bathroom is,
there I was finding the loophole
in chain-link, as if I'd never grown to be
                                    5' 11", never learned
to open a bottle of beer with my teeth.
Soo-ling, Soo-ling. What were the neighbors to make
of a nineteen-year-old boy moaning outside their doors,
whispering into their rose bushes?
                                    Soo-ling, SOO-ling
I, who could recite Wittgenstein's Fifth Corollary
in German and do entire calculus problems in my head,

was calling in a voice so high
that you'd never imagine I could have brought a girl   .
to climax three times
                              in one night.
What was the point of taking Psychology 101
if I was going to lose my wits
and the tail of my shirt in the barbed wire some rich person put up
to keep people like me off his estate?
By now I was so far from home
I didn't even have a clue whose yard I was crossing,
the way I used to at nine when I didn't care
who owned what,
                              it had been all mine
to wage war on. I'd been too busy battling Germans
to read No Trespass signs. Now
I was pushing aside branches with the sheer force
of my running, throwing myself into brambles
as if nothing had a right
to get in my way, I made it my mission
to rescue this Siamese even if she was determined
not to be rescued.
                              Incursion
after incursion till the dark couldn't possibly
refuse me, and if it did, there was no justice
to be had. *It's just a cat. Not even purebred.*
Not really mine, I kept telling myself, as I peered under wet leaves,
down snake holes. I'd go underground
after her, if I had to, save her
                              despite herself.
It was not that long before
the president would order the first bombings
and I'd meet a girl who'd cry so softly into the phone
right then and there, on the other end of the line
                              I'd decide to marry her.
But now, all that was on my mind was the cry
of a cat so forlorn, she must have known
that the world was ending and there'd be nothing
any of us could do to stop the sky from darkening.

The World of Business

Marcel Proust on Marketing.
Instructions to the Jesuit Brothers Who Manage Haciendas.
George Washington and Truth in Advertising.
Open to any page of the boxed set and there is my father:
talking to Emperor Hadrian or John Wanamaker,
Alexander Hamilton or Bernal Diaz Del Castillo.

My dad could turn anyone into an entrepreneur.
Hitler, Gandhi. No one was safe from my old man:
Stalin's excerpted speech was retitled "New Methods of Work,
New Methods of Management,"
even George Bernard Shaw ended up a poster boy
for life insurance. Tarquin the Proud, Lorenzo de Medici,

Haile Selassie, Boss Tweed, and Dwight David Eisenhower crowded
into my father's thirty-page index, that great hall
where he'd brought together the world's leaders
so they might agree on certain principles: the healing efficacy
of hard work, the virtues of enlightened
self-interest. It is 1964. My father is at his desk
in his mistress's house, just learning

to drink enough to put everything painful out of his head:
his disappointing son, his crazy wife.
He ends his four-volume labor with what he calls *a challenge*
for the second half of our twentieth century
and for the rest of the years that lie ahead waiting for man
to fill them with his busy dreaming
and his busy doing. By the time of publication

those millions my father envisioned
buying *The World of Business*
would have better things to do; boys sent home

in body bags, the country heavily invested in a war
by men not even mentioned in any of the 1135 pages.
If they'd just read my books, my father liked to say,
as if apologizing to everyone indexed in *The World of Business.*

Buddha, Carnegie, Herodotus, Conrad Hilton,
J. Pierpont Morgan, Michelangelo, the prophet Mohammed
knew the importance of consumer research and good PR.
A failure in marketing strategy, he'd sigh
as he'd sweeten his drink. Yes, most of the world's problems
could be attributed to that: *bad marketing.*
It had much to answer for.

The Great Society

While the president was upstairs promising
America and our fraternity television
that he'd bring an end to poverty in our lifetime,
in the cellar our minds were, at that moment, on something else
much more important: a woman
who was taking off her clothes
in what we liked to call the Cave
because that made all thirty-five of us animals.
Half of us were virgins but we loved to talk
about eating pussy and we said it so often
we almost forgot that we'd never seen a real vagina
much less put our tongue in one.
But that didn't stop us that night
that LBJ appeared in millions of living rooms
to explain just how he'd accomplish
what Lincoln hadn't been able to.
Nor did it stop our evening's star from slipping off her bra
and letting her bosoms talk
to the kid who was studying to be a psychiatrist,
the French major, the boy who loved to play chopsticks
all day on the fraternity piano
instead of going to Organic Chemistry.
When she peeled off her stockings
her thighs made obvious
what we'd been trying not to notice:
she was older than some of our mothers,
her hair bleached so thoroughly it looked sprayed on,
and try as we could to lust after her
it was like wanting to make love to our grandmothers.
We could hear Lyndon upstairs declaring war
on poverty as our four-hundred-dollar stripper peeled off her panties
and then what else could we gaze at
but her groin, that dark tangle of threads

someone had forgotten to clip
after they'd finished sewing up a wound.
My fellow Americans, we have just begun
to glimpse what is possible,
the thirty-sixth president of the United States was saying upstairs
as downstairs this woman each of us had paid
a week's allowance to watch disrobe to nothing but skin
called us up to the stage, one by one,
and undid the history major's belt
and slipped down his boxers
and there was his penis as interested in the event
as a worm at the Battle of Hastings,
and then she made the mechanical engineer drop his pants
but there was only a little to work with
and much less to operate on
with the pre-med, and even the kid we liked to call Rock
was soft and the boy nicknamed Beastie,
and the phonograph record she'd brought with her
seemed louder than it had before
till even her music was laughing at us
and none of us said a word
when she put on her robe and counted the money
and got out the door
before we realized she'd taken the twenty-dollar scotch
we'd been saving for after finals
and so we went back to doing what we had to:
pass Calculus, pass Foundations of Education,
pass Human Anatomy II, pass Abnormal Psychology,
pass U.S. History: The War Years,
so we could be ready to join the Great Society.

1964

A decade after
a forty-three-year-old black woman's feet grew too tired
to pay attention to realpolitik
and she sat down in the very seat reserved for her
by fate and made the bus famous and broke more
than one law
and not quite a decade before
the night a gaggle of men who primped and loved
what they became in front of mirrors
hitched up their skirts and pummeled the living daylights
out of not just New York's finest
but history,
and 1931 years
since the alarm with no snooze button,
that damn rooster,
disturbed the peace and the party hack, the Apostle Peter,
woke up in a sweat, not sure
that he'd picked the right man
to support and so turned his back
on his candidate and his cross,
on a badly lit side road,
Christopher, a boy noted for his cowardice, on and off
the field, got up the nerve to take
history into his hands and began unbuttoning
a girl's blouse, and miracle
of miracles, she not only let him
but guided his fingers
down into her panties. You'd have thought
he'd discovered gold in Africa or jumped out of a
plane, the way he bragged afterwards
to the dark—he had to tell someone
what it was like to fall
straight out of the sky

and all day he smelled the dark continent on his fingertips
and nothing changed in the world
because a kid in a parked car one August evening
decided to be brave, and yet everything did.
            Take my word for it.

3

For matter, all heaped up and clogged, would lie,
Settled in heaviness, age upon endless age,
But as it is, no quiet is granted the atoms,
The first-beginnings; there is no bottom to
The world, where they might flow and take their rest. . . .
In fact, Nature herself constrains the world
From granting itself a limit. She forces the atoms
To be bounded by a void and to bound the void in turn.

De Rerum Natura, Book One

January 19, 1972

Once you can't get out of your head
that the house may be in danger of bursting into fire
you must check the oven, iron, every lampshade in every room
twice. Not that long ago
your wife forgot to turn off the gas under a pan.
Not that long ago you dropped a cigarette into the sofa
and now each time you sit down, you hear the smoke alarm.
Just last week, the neighbor's furnace blew.
The worst part of having panic disorder
is that there are so many good reasons
for panic. When you had your baby, you didn't suspect
that you'd end up loving this child
so much that he'd be your ticket
not away from terrors but to even more.
At night you wake in a burning village
searching for your baby, though he's still sleeping
in the bassinet beside you. Then it's your best friend
you're searching for, though he'd been sent home from Vietnam
early, only wounded
a little. Even in the hallway to the psychiatrist's office
you wonder if what you notice
is really just a truck riding its brakes
or the wind carried from the Route 128 incinerator.
Should you push the buzzer to let the doctor know?
What if he's with another patient?
So you open a magazine and pretend
to be interested in its yachts and home-repair projects.
Maybe your mind's just tricking your nose.
You have, after all, been clinically diagnosed
as making much too much of things.
Even though you're more and more sure
that's smoke you're detecting,
you let the doctor lead you down the hall
to his double doors, and not till you're halfway

through a dream does the doctor ask if you smell anything.
Why, now that you mention it, I do,
you say and then you are all outside:
anorexics, obsessive compulsives, bedwetters, and mood disorders
with your doctors, and the smoke's inside
rummaging through files, charging from room to room
as if it'd just bought the place
and was inspecting what it had purchased.
For someone who's trying to convince himself
that the world is not about to go up in flames
an episode like this is surely a setback.

Singing Yourself Down the Stairs

How long can this young man hold his club over my head
before his arm grows so tired, he's got to
bring it down, let it do
                    what it was meant to do,
teach the back of my neck a lesson it won't
soon forget?
                    No Blood for Oil!
What was I thinking when I made the sign?
That the cops would read
what I'd written and go and tell the president?
                    No more napalm!
No more body bags! Was I foolish enough to believe
that people at home getting supper, singing
to their babies, running the bath water,
would glance up at their television sets
and see words held high on sticks
and say, *Oh yes, we have to change our lives!*
Maybe the cop who's looking straight at me
as if he'd kill me if he could
                    get away with it
did the same thing as I did last night: sang
his son in and out of his bath
and then sang himself down the stairs,
no different from any father
who, having argued with the shadows in his child's room,
wants the last word and
                    that word to be song
not because singing makes the dark
any less dark, the cold less determined to
infiltrate our bones, not because song wins
any concessions from a congress
of cancer cells or has any hope of bringing
peace on earth, but because words, by themselves, are
not enough. The only god I could tolerate

would be one who sings
        to himself,
part guffaw, part trembling, part whistle,
part wail because it's the only way he can
bear all the empty places he can't fill, the unrelenting,
        infinitely
irreconcilable universe. And so the father sings.
        And so the son.

Why I Hate Math

The day my daughter was hit by a car
approximately 38,550 children died of hunger and hunger-
related diseases. It didn't matter how many times
her mother and I had warned her
about the street. Being four and so enchanted
by her game, she forgot
that anything could hurt her,
especially the car that did. I wouldn't speak of this
if she'd been killed. I am not one of the unlucky
parents who did all they could to keep their children
safe, only to lose a son
or daughter anyway. To what?
Cancer? Spinal Meningitis? Famine? War? Accident?
The laws of percentages?
Some nights the house gets so dark
I have to claw my way out of
a dream and bump against sofa, piano, bookcase
to my daughter's room. I used to be secretly glad
my wife couldn't breast-feed.
I loved the kiss of the first few drops from the bottle
on my wrist, the little reassuring
scalding that reminded me that even though I was half-asleep,
I was doing my best to make sure that it was me
that got burned, not my child.
At 3 a.m. I'd hold the baby
so tight it was almost as if she were drinking
from my body. All my shirts smelled
of milk and spit-up. In the middle of a difficult meeting
or stuck in traffic, all I had to do was breathe
deeply, and Nora would be so real
I'd look down, surprised
she wasn't in my arms. I labored under the assumption
that if I tried my hardest, life would
reward me, keep the pavement from bruising my child,

the fire from leaping off the stove,
lightning from striking. I learned
what all parents must: All the worry, all the vigilance
in a moment cancelled out and there's nothing
one can do. One might as well try to argue with an equation.
No court of appeal, no retribution.
Just ruthless algebra.

August 6

Lie down on the street! I tell my son
so he takes off his jacket
and methodically, the way he's learned at Cub Scouts,
folds it smaller and smaller, like a flag,
and then it turns into a pillow.
My daughter, usually wanting nothing more
than to do what her brother just did,
follows his example and folds her hands so tightly over her chest,
the left and the right seem afraid
to let go of each other. We look up at the clouds
and wait for them to tell us something
they haven't yet. The street is full of bodies
pretending to be stricken, trying to
be as dead as they can, though soon my son grows bored
with his own dying and is ready to
get back to what no one can beat him at:
systematically, ingeniously
tormenting his sister and then teasing her even more
for crying. Then a siren tears open the heavens.
The doves, set loose, swirl above us, dive and rise
as if the earth's on fire and there's nowhere
safe to alight. My son stretches his hand up
into the air. My daughter does the same.
If her brother's just done it, then it must be important to do.
It's obvious that they can't grasp anything
but air, though when did that ever stop a kid
from reaching his arm up
to pluck a hawk from the clouds,
seize a shooting star? That old lie of perspective, deceit
of vision, one more betrayal
kids never get used to. On the stage
a man with no legs is embracing a man
with no eyes, but we are gazing past them to the darkening sky.

Today we hold it responsible
not only for the storm about to scatter us,
the cops fidgety as winds and just as trigger happy,
but for everything gone wrong in the universe.

Politics Ends When You Unwrap a Sandwich

After a whole morning of looking at each other,
it was almost impossible for either side not to crack
jokes. We plied the cops with raisins and sunflower seeds
and they offered us sticks of gum and Tic Tacs.
It's what I imagined might happen
if two armies came to rest on two banks
of a river, the call to attack postponed
so long, they'd get tired
of glowering at each other and begin to drink
the same water, and skip rocks
where the river grows narrow, even get caught up
trying to splash the other side
as if that were the only good way to fight a war.
It didn't take much to disperse us
any more than it would waves to dispose of their debris,
though like any flotsam and jetsam
we kept drifting back
and kept being swept away.
Some of the younger cops even made a game
out of grabbing a few of us and letting us
wriggle free. We'd inch close, then leap back,
the way kids at the beach try the sea's patience
testing their youth against its years
of experience, as if this huge monolith was just a pal
they were free to tease. It's easy to forget the ocean's dark
intentions, its immense leverage, its weight
of authority. Kids claw their way out of the surf
they'd thought was only playing with them.
They rise indignant as if the sea's at fault
for swallowing them. That's how some of us reacted
as we choked on the gas,
as the same men we'd kidded just moments before
threw us to the ground and dug their knees into our backs.

The cop whose son was a jazz pianist?
The cop whose daughter was pre-med?
The cop one month from retirement?
We couldn't tell one club from the other.

No Verifiable Proof

When they showed us the severed hand
we thought that it was just one more
of their hoaxes. After all, it was not really a hand

but a photograph, and pictures may be worth more
than a thousand words, but often they are just
lies. So they brought us a chopped-off head

to verify it, just a mouth, and who doesn't know
what a mouth is capable of? More
fabrications. And this mouth was grinning

as if the joke was on us. Then they produced a wing
from a man's back, but it was merely more
bone, and even the biggest fools recognize that dead men

exaggerate. If they couldn't convince us with one skull
why did they imagine that two would do? Usually more
is less. A good liar knows when to shut up.

But they brought us more. Not just one tongue, but a whole
sack of them, each with its own story. How gullible
did they think us? All those tongues, those fibs?

After they pulled ears out of their pockets
did they expect us to take them seriously? Fingers, toes,
noses? So many they were obviously more

concoctions. But we'd grown exasperated by then,
the way parents get after their children keep telling more
and bigger whoppers. Even after a child guesses

his mother knows that he's lying, he'll go on
with his story. He's committed to it. He owes it more
than lip service. Here's a jawbone. Here's a shinbone.

Here's what we already suspected: the whole
is not more than the sum of its parts.
A Hutu here. A Tutsi. A Serb here. A Croatian there.

Just one more exercise in postmodern deconstruct-
ionalism. Bring me your severed hand
and tell me that the pain is more than you can bear

and you and I both know of what you are guilty:
gratuitous distortion of the facts. Here a lopped-off ear.
There a skull laughing at us for swallowing

its own propaganda: that it ever mattered
to a body that had let go of it more quickly than you'd
have supposed. Maybe the belly got tired

of the brain's compulsive lying? Or the groin had better things
to do than put up with the head's exhausting self-
importance? When they brought us a penis

that was the last straw. When they started talking rape,
that was more than we could stand. That they'd lie
about something as awful as genocide, expect us

to believe humans capable, more than once
in their lifetimes, of holocaust. If there'd been a slaughter
that remarkable, wouldn't we be the first to know?

College Professor Suspended

Semulkahn, three years away from her native Liberia,
bends over her blue book
with the concentration of someone trying to land a plane
in a pasture. Stochko, the paraplegic,
wears Hawaiian shirts so outrageous
he's obviously making a point:
so what if I'm in a wheelchair?
I still can be as gorgeous as a tropical bird.
Ankit presses so close to his exam book, it's a door
he's trying to push open.
Winston lifts his head, takes a gulp of air,
and then dives back into his essay.
So what if he can't speak a simple sentence
without stuttering? Rachel,
the kid who spent the last ten years in foster care,
jumps on her midterm
as someone might on a horse she intends to ride hard
into the sunset. Every few minutes
she digs her spurs in. Peter's tossing his hair back.
It keeps getting between him
and what he wants to say. It's so dark and wavy
all the girls want to run their fingers
through it. Even the teacher has all he can do
to keep his hands out of its tangles.
Why should it shock anyone that a teacher might wish to
lie down with one of his students?
The girl whispering to the words she writes
as if to coax them out of hiding.
The boy who's said nothing all term
but whose thoughts rush onto the paper now
like water out of a faucet, spilling over, reveling in the fact
of all this empty space, the unexpected freedom
of the page. The heroin addict.
The baseball pitcher, who one day confesses to the class

his dad's a drunk. *That's why I never tell him
the day I'm gonna start.*
The girl who's got gum stuck in her hair.
The pimply kid who strokes his ankle as he writes,
the one smooth part
left to his body. *All that nakedness
mine*, thinks the teacher.

The Congressman from Bucks County Answers a Question

For some it's second nature, brushing a fly
from your face or squishing an ant about to
take a shortcut over your sandwich.
You really don't mean any more harm to the insect
than the congressman did. It wasn't his job
to consider whether or not it took courage for a girl
with bad acne and a worse overbite
to stand up before every single person in school
and ask a question
of the chairman of the House Subcommittee on Investigations
who'd only a few weeks ago had his picture taken
climbing out of the just-deposed dictator's bunker
grinning as men do, posing
beside big fish they intend to mount on their walls.
The congressman had been a social worker
so he'd had long practice at putting people
in their place and did it to her
in such a casual way he wouldn't have to think
about it afterward—the way you'd nudge a dog out of your path
or tease a little brother to tears
because he's stupid enough to keep pestering you.
Everyone couldn't help laughing. Even the congressman
smiled at his own joke. Surely the student knew better
than to expect an apology
from a man elected to office by 78,342 votes.
How do you win a fight with a man the papers never tire of
photographing? What's newsworthy about a girl
so upset by a war that she reads everything
she can about it and risks making a fool of herself
in front of boys to whom she'd never dared to speak,
groups of girls she'll have to pass in the halls,
teachers in whose classes she's spent years
trying to be invisible? Now she's trying to move
as little of her body as possible,

to stand up straight and devote all her attention
to this important man doing his best
to pretend she's not still staring at him.
Maybe if she had resisted the cops
as they dragged her away
somebody would have gotten up and rushed to her rescue,
but everyone stayed in their seats
as if this was just part of the show they'd been summoned to:
an important person surrounded by bodyguards
and an unimportant person led away.

Utopia

> In the next fifty minutes create a perfect world.
> Be sure to proofread.

So what if their utopias occasionally drop the ending
for the past tense or dangle participles,
at least they will have managed, all by themselves
in the next hour,
                        to cure cancer and AIDS,
and if the sentences in which they distribute wealth equally,
clean up the rivers, wipe out racism,
and put an end to crime as well as invent a drug
that's not addictive or expensive, but just as eye opening
as LSD, and, while they're at it, outlaw
political parties and final exams,
                        run on,
what's the big deal? Your students aren't interested
in anything as petty as punctuation.
In the kingdom created by the girl
whose grandmother has been dying all semester,
no one uses semicolons and everyone gets to
turn into whatever they wish. *It's not like reincarnation,*
she writes. *You get to remember your past existence*
and you go back to being who you were
if you're tired of being a lizard or a lake.
                        No one hurts anyone
in the anorexic's utopia, but if they do
they get nails driven into their palms
and are hung in the city square.
                        Ask for imagination
and expect consistency? For the president of the Young Republicans,
top priority is equality. In his planetary nudist colony
everyone's forbidden to wear a stitch of clothes.
The marketing major's a hermit. The art major wants money
harvested like marijuana, field after field

of hundred-dollar bills. He grows fabulously wealthy
right before your eyes.
                        No matter how often
you write *See me!* on the essays
of the young man who always is talking about Jesus,
you can't get him to stick to a thesis.
There is no such thing as expository writing
in his heaven. Its valleys are verdant green.
He's not worried about redundancy
or apostrophes in paradise.
                        Utopia
for the kid just out of reform school
is the backwoods behind a quarry
where he's free to ride dirt bikes and dive off cliffs.
The water's torn and heals itself
all day. Maybe it's not the end of the world
if he can't get *their* and *there* straight.
                        After the class
the kid who always wears his Yankees hat backwards
lifts his shirt to show you exactly where,
on his stomach,
                        the medicine gets pumped in.
His utopia brims with light
the color of insulin. His roads have no traffic.

Thanksgiving Will Never Be the Same

> Thomas Granger, servant to an honest man of Duxbury, of
> 16 or 17 years of age, was this year detected of buggery, and
> indicted for the same.
>
> William Bradford.

To get boys interested
in the Pilgrims, book II, chapter XXXII, anno Dom. 1642
of Governor Bradford's journal
ought to do the trick. Does one use a step stool
to have sex with a horse, whisper sweet nothings
in the cow's ear? How much foreplay
is required by a goat? Certainly that year the turkey got a different kind of stuffing.
Horrible it is to mention,
One William Spence accidentally saw the boy's lewd practices
with a ewe (I forbear particulars).
The pronouns' coupling.
That coy parenthesis. Its double entendre.
You could almost accuse the good governor of being a postmodernist.
Maybe even a deconstructionalist!
And whereas
some of the sheep could not be so well known
by first description of them, others
were brought straight before the accused
and he declared which were they and which were not.
What's endearing
is that the boy compliantly identified which of the flock
he'd been intimate with, picked out each
by her smell, the sweet, greasy lanolin
deep within each fiber, the spring
to each coil, the fleece's welcoming
congregation of curls, their unconditional
surrender.
And, accordingly,
he was cast by the jury and condemned,
the 8th of September, 1642. A very sad spectacle it was.

For first the mare and then the cow and the rest of the lesser cattle
were killed, before the youth's face,
according to the law, Leviticus, XX 15, and then the youth himself
was executed and all cast into
a great and large pit.

     O America,
God shed his grace on thee.

The Soul Wants the Last Word

If you can't trust me, whom can you
                trust? says
        the soul, that bully
with his Bhagavad Gita,
                that Jungian therapist,
        transcendental
thug, maharishi
                in circus tights
        who's tricked you up so high
you can't get down.
                Let yourself go,
        says the *Here*.
What are you waiting for?
                asks the *Now*.
        Meaning: jump in the water
though it's miles over your head.
                Meaning: open the door
        of the airplane
and see if the air respects your self-
                actualization.
        You've got to live
in the moment,
                says the soul.
        It's got wings
and is ready
                to take you
        for a ride.
So what if you can't breathe?
                So what
        if there's too much light
to see? It's put on sunglasses.
                It's turned up the music.
        Don't look down,
it says. *Whatever you do*
                don't
        look down.

Farewell Ceremony

Tell the fifteen-year-old who flunked gym
because he couldn't imagine his body doing anything
but falling
      that thirty years later
he'd be handing out diplomas to carjackers
and coke-dealers, pimps, and pickpockets.
      Today
that goofball who made a habit
of walking into walls
when girls passed him in the hallways
      gathers in a circle:
Gloria, who cut her stepdad's throat,
Steph, the dazzlingly beautiful, self-taught safecracker,
Sylvia who keeps getting arrested for
      dumb shit!
You think I'm ever going to learn?
Tonight the one who hands her a piece of paper
that says she did
      is the same person
who dropped out of school because he got tired
of having his head shoved into toilets.
      Tonight, at this,
their last meeting, Big Tony stops hitting
on whatever female hasn't already told him to fuck off
      and grows silent
for the moment it takes him to light
his neighbor's candle, tipping it slightly
      to wish godspeed
to Speedo, the cat burglar,
who looks as if he can't decide whether or not to laugh
at the candles' feeble attempts to fill the whole room
with light, each flame's brief gesture
      of solicitude.

The purse snatcher scolds the D.U.I.,
Stay loose, stay cool and out of traffic school.
The crackhead cautions the smash-and-grabber,
Don't scratch that itch,
                    as he pulls flame out of nothing
but wax and thread, that ordinary marvel,
the room so quiet
you can almost hear the wicks
                    burning.

42 Linden

Live! Learn! Worship! Shop!
The Paradise Chamber of Commerce

1

The Promised Land Mall. The Elysian Fields Spa.
The Shangri-la Delicatessen.
Of course it got out of hand. Who wouldn't want to
make a buck or two off the other world?
Take a right at Celestial, go straight past Olympus,
Valhalla, and Nirvana
and you can't miss Harry's Heavenly Hotdogs.
Galilee Plastics. River Jordan Wingnuts.
Mount Sinai Waste Management Corp.
Who wouldn't find the ironies delicious
if Paradise had more than its share
of embezzlers, check forgers, inside traders, wives
who sleep with their gardeners?
Mostly, though, it's just a working-class community.
Children, tired of their homework, listen to acid rock
while they load and unload their fathers' collections of antique guns,
and everyone goes on being born
and dying at the appointed times on Apostle Drive
or the Blessed Martyrs Boulevard.

2

As soon as their wives and kids drive off to church,
the men on streets named after trees and flowers and fruits
head for the cellar and their train sets, the hills
they've molded so softly rolling to the sea
that not even God could have done a better job.
On the seventh day none of them rest; instead

they search the house for the right screwdriver,
the precise size of wrench. Every week
comes down to this: oiling the tiny gears
that keep the world and its railroads running.
The milk car must deliver its miniature silver cans at 48 Fleur-De-Lis.
The cattle car has a quota it must honor on 76 Hyacinth.
Tiny sacks of mail. Tiny logs. Tinier coal.
Beneath 42 Linden's house too, there are rails
to be laid, mountains to be raised,
tunnels to be dug.
Fields expect their fair share of flowers;
rivers demand to be carved out of the land.
The sun must be set in the heavens
and the moon can't wait. It's got to make sure
that the tides come in and go out on schedule.

3

Imagine buying up so much land
you'd be free to name every body of water, every hill
on it, turn what was a Sodom and Gomorrah
of sumac and poison ivy
into a heaven on which anyone could put down a deposit,
uproot the degeneracy of vines, their illicit embraces.
Whoever laid out the traffic patterns in Paradise
didn't want to leave anything to chance:
in the Nightingale section every street begins with N;
with an O in Oriole Glen; in Periwinkle no road's allowed
if it doesn't start with P and from there you turn into Quail Hollow,
then Rambling Rose, then Snowball Gate,
and then Tamarisk. What fun
to be in charge of the language, to have the alphabet
all one's own to do with as one wishes.

4

It's not April, yet at 44 Linden Drive a boy's
already half-naked, on the theory,
perhaps, that if he acts like it's spring,
then spring will get the picture
and come when the boy wants it, which is now,
shooting hoops in his driveway
in a town someone had the hubris to name
Paradise. He could be any one of a number of boys
tired of gravity, making free throws against his father's garage,
but right now he's the savior
in gym shorts, leading his people out of Egypt
as the ball finds its way back
to the promised land. What's sweeter
than hitting nothing but strings?
The bonus to a jump shot: watching it
jostle the net, the space still filled
by what's just fallen through it, that lovely illusion
of closure, and the boy wants it
again and again, and he'll shoot layups, finger rolls, skyhooks
till he gets it back, no pleasure ever enough,
even in Paradise.

5

When he lived in the city, Apt. 3B grew so used to worrying
that it stopped being worry. It's what he did:
he woke the kids up, got their breakfast,
saw to it that they brushed their teeth,
and pulled them out of the way of oncoming cars.
But now he's 42 Linden Drive
and here the streets have such pretty names:
Lily of the Valley Lane, Honey Locust Hollow.
It's a wonder cars dare drive down them.
Maybe he moved here because he believed
in the power of language. If his kids played on streets

named Frankincense, Sandalwood, Quince
and all in a town called Paradise
how could any irreparable harm befall them?
What does it matter if Quince doesn't thrive
in these parts, if there is no Persimmon
on Persimmon Court? Mahogany Road, Rosewood Drive,
Teak Court, no day complete without the elegant furnishings
of trees, their dark, alluvial grains.

6

Night after night 42 Linden stands just outside
his children's room and because he can't hear anything
listens even harder, convinced that it's out there—
whatever wants to hurt his kids—
and he's got to be ready to throw himself in front of it,
whatever it is. What if he were to screw up
and lose his job and have to explain to his children
why they must say goodbye to gardens
and golf courses? So 42 Linden never rests.
The way a blade of grass, every second of every minute,
reminds itself not to loosen its grip
on its little piece of property. The way a babbling brook works
its full-time job rushing the same direction
day in and day out. You can't be too careful.
Even in Paradise. Especially in Paradise.

7

Sometimes the worry gets too much for 42 Linden
and so he makes up excuses
to get up from the floor where he's been crayoning
with his kids. There's something broken he's been meaning to fix.
The boy next door is jumping into the sky
and it takes 42 Linden a moment
to realize that the kid's just snagging a rebound.

The kid's shoulders glisten. Today he's not skin and bones
that happened to get bad grades in algebra
and have acne. Today the sun turns every blotch on the boy's face
irrelevant. Day and night he's out there
throwing a ball against the rim,
sometimes even trying to miss, teaching his hands
what to do when he's way off the mark.
The boy never seems to get tired of chasing down his mistakes.
He seems born to do this: scoop up a ball in his hands
and lift off the earth as if he knows
that this is the closest he's ever going to come to having wings.

8

On Monday 42 Linden Drive packs lunches for his kids;
On Tuesday he leads his Cub Scouts in the Pledge of Allegiance;
On Wednesday he marks his students'
essays: B+, B/B-, C+, A++.
The crazy enterprise of pretending that one can
put a grade on anything.
Thursday he takes a neighbor to the hospital
while her husband's out on the lawn shouting
he's learned his lesson, he won't do it again.
On Friday 42 Linden gets home early so he can leave his wife
at her job at the lab and pick up the kids
and still have time with them, at dusk,
to throw stones into the river
till everything grows dark and finally they can see
distances only by hearing them, the splash each rock makes.

9

Put in Paradise, how many of us wouldn't return
to our old occupations: if you were a burglar,
testing the locks, trying the windows;
if you were a retired plumber, making work

out of the smallest of jobs;
if you're a father doing what you do best, worrying;
if you were a child of an alcoholic, second-guessing
everything, undermining your best intentions?
That night 42 Linden's wife moves her hands over him
with the quiet authority of water,
the way water's able to find every hollow
and crevice and fill it, and yet no matter how grateful
42 Linden is, his mind wanders.
Now it's the furious self-importance
of a stone skimmed over a creek.
Now, it's the sound of pages being flipped,
his four-year-old daughter's ritual
after she's been kissed goodnight and the door's closed,
reading book after book
till she falls asleep in mid-sentence.
Now it's the way the ball keeps persuading the strings
to let it drop through the exact center,
the way a kid's already under the net waiting
for his last shot to fall back into his hands
as if it's never enough to do something perfectly
just once, you've got to do it again
and again. Even as 42 Linden's wife seems to pour herself
over him, even as he opens his legs
to take her in, he can hear the ball bouncing
off the rim. Is it all right
in Paradise to go on dreaming of still another paradise?
That's what 42 Linden would like to know.
He's a child being rescued from a sinking ship.
He's a boy carried off by a bird
and set down in the lap of the clouds.
He's a young man plummeting through a sky
so immense he could fall forever.

DE RERUM NATURA

> ... the funeral song is mingled
> With the cry of babies come to the shores of light

It's the perfect book if you're thinking of killing yourself,
but don't really want to. If you'd like to
believe in God but find Him
even more daunting than that erector set
you got one Christmas, all those complicated instructions
when really all you wanted to do was
screw one shiny metal thing to another. If despair's
your only true principle, if you're convinced
that the world's an awful place,
Lucretius won't try to sway you
from your allegiances. He provides more than enough
pestilence, war, disease
to satisfy the most confirmed pessimist:
The throat oozes black blood, the tongue drips gore,
The dogs stretch flat on the street and lay down their sick souls,
And the bodies of lifeless parents are heaped
On the lifeless bodies of children.
Yet right after *the temples become charnel houses*
there Lucretius is, on the next page,
giving a lecture on meteorology, saying *Gee whiz*
in Latin, like the biggest dork on earth,
a professor so excited about his lab experiment
he stops worrying whether the students are awake
or not. He can't get over the vacuum
that makes life so interesting:
how the atoms have to keep filling it
in new and unpredictable ways. If you want a reason
to go on living, even in the midst
of a long and protracted war, it's the magnet,
stone at which you gape in wonder . . .
You can link rings in a chain suspended from it,
And sometimes you'll see five or even more

Dangle in order and sway in the light breeze
One ring depending on the next, as each
Communicates with the magnet's binding force
And cling— such potency seeps through them all.
Once you get Lucretius started,
there's no stopping him. He's like a kid fallen
so in love that nothing makes sense now
except in reference to the one he's besotted with. *Magnets!*
Remember those little dogs
that kids used to play with, pulling the white terrier
from the black, then making it fly smack into the other
as if there were no end to the pleasure
of investigation: hypotheses you had to keep testing over and over,
the air first charged with the power
of refusal, then the irresistible embrace, north seeking south.
south seeking north, crazed lovers,
the urgent kiss of metal
against metal? Were these little Scotties
really teaching boys and girls the facts of life?
Maybe kids wouldn't get so screwed up
if they kept up their religious studies
of magnetism. After all, Lucretius died only a few years
before Christ was born. Maybe the cross
is a kind of magnet. Drugs are, surely. And porn.
Maybe it's not just okay to be pulled
toward the very thing that you know
you must resist. Maybe
it's a law of physics. Open *De Rerum Natura*
to Book Six, if you are not sure
that life's worth living, if you're torn this way and that.
Look, Lucretius says, it's all possible
because there's so much space
to be filled and it gets really crowded
with all those plagues and priests
telling everyone what to believe. *But—*
how the author of *The Nature of Things* loves this word—
consider how porous it all is,
how there's always room

for atoms to do what they have their hearts set
on doing: finding windows
to slip in and out of, *secret passages,*
whole highways, pipes up our Roman troublemaker,
in a thing that looked so solid
nothing could get through, doors flung open
where no doors seem possible.

Acknowledgments

The author is grateful to the following magazines in which the poems from this manuscript previously appeared: *Bellingham Review* ("E Pluribus Unum"); *Manhattan Review* ("The Barbarians," "Irreconcilable Differences," "Nothing More Dangerous than Boredom," "What Do You Hate about Yourself," and "Why Latin Should Still Be Taught"); *New Letters* ("August 6," "College Professor Suspended," "Politics Ends," "Thanksgiving," and "Trying to Keep Things in Perspective"); and *Sun* ("*De Rerum Natura*" and "42 Linden Drive," under the name "Model Community").

Quotations from Lucretius come from *Of the Nature of Things*, translated by Anthony M. Esolen. Copyright 1995. Reprinted with the permission of The Johns Hopkins University Press.

The Donald Hall Prize money has been donated to A Woman's Place, Bucks County Community College Foundation, Family Services of Bucks County's Quality of Life AIDS Project, the Red Cross Homeless Shelter, and the American Anti-Slavery Group.

This manuscript would not be possible without the guidance of Steven Huff, Lynn Levin, George Drew, Pam and Herb Perkins-Frederick, Pam Bernard, Charles Harper Webb, and the Vermont College Postgraduate Writers' Conference Manuscript Workshop. I am grateful for the inspiration of the Spring Poetry Workshop, the continued support of my colleague Helen Lawton Wilson, the wise counsel of Peter Bridge and Dr. Rona Cohen, and the abiding love from my wife, Mary Ann, and my children.